The Ultimate Crepe Recipe Book!

Delicious Crepe Recipes You Have to Try Out!

BY: Valeria Ray

License Notes

Copyright © 2019 Valeria Ray All Rights Reserved

All rights to the content of this book are reserved by the Author without exception unless permission is given stating otherwise.

The Author have no claims as to the authenticity of the content and the Reader bears all responsibility and risk when following the content. The Author is not liable for any reparations, damages, accidents, injuries or other incidents occurring from the Reader following all or part of this publication.

Table of Contents

Introduction 6

1. Basic buttermilk crepes.. 7

2. Brownie crepes 10

3. Sweet potato crepes.. 13

4. Oatmeal crepes 15

5. Coconut crepes with poppy and cinnamon cream 18

6. Cheese crepes 21

7. S'more's crepes 24

8. Banana bread crepes... 26

9. Mac and cheese crepes 29

10. Strawberry cheesecake crepes 32

11. Dark chocolate crepe 35

12. Pumpkin spice crepes 38

13. Gingerbread crepes... 40

14. Chocolate chip crepes 43

15. Oreo crepes 46

16. Biscoff crepes 49

17. Apple pie crepes 53

18. Nutella crepes 57

19. Ham and cheese hash brown crepes 59

20. French toast crepes 62

21. Blueberry crepes 64

22. Tropical mango crepes 67

23. Butter crepes with chocolate hazelnut filling 69

24. Belgian chocolate crepes 72

25. Hazelnut crepes with cinnamon yogurt 74

26. Maple and bacon crepes 77

27. Pecan pie crepes 80

28. Fried chicken crepes 83

29. Pizza crepes 88

30. Sand crepes with cinnamon sugar 90

Conclusion 93

About the Author 94

Author's Afterthoughts 96

Introduction

Soft, fluffy and absolutely delicious! Crepes are a delicious breakfast option. But why stop there? Crepes for dinner? Yes please! This recipe book brings you a medley of sweet and savory crepes that can be made anytime, anywhere! So let's dive right in!

1. Basic buttermilk crepes

Make this recipe the base for your own crepe creations. You can fold in pretty much anything into this batter and you can serve these yummy crepes topped with any fruit or sugary sauce you like.

Total time: 20m

Servings: 4

Ingredients:

- 2 cup buttermilk
- 3 tsp vanilla
- 4 tsp baking powder
- 1 3/4 cup flour
- 3 tbsp. Sugar
- ½ cup butter, melted
- 2 eggs

Instructions:

1. Preheat your pan on high.

2. Combine the dry ingredients in a bowl.

3. Whisk together the wet ones in another.

4. Gently combine the two mixtures.

5. Spoon of the batter onto a hot, greased pan, and spread thin.

6. Cook for about 2 minutes, or until golden.

7. Repeat with the remaining batter.

8. Serve with your favorite toppings and enjoy!

2. Brownie crepes

If you're a fan of brownies, then these are probably going to be your favorite crepe recipe! Serve with whipped cream and vanilla ice cream!

Total time: 15m

Servings: 12

Ingredients:

- 1 ¼ cups of all-purpose flour
- ½ cup of powdered cocoa, unsweetened
- 1 cup of white sugar
- 1 tsp. Of baking powder
- 1 tsp. Of sea salt
- 10 tbsp. Of butter, melted
- 2 eggs
- 2 tsp. Of pure vanilla
- 1/3 cup of water
- 2/3 cups of miniature chocolate chips
- Vanilla ice cream, for serving
- Icing sugar, for topping

Instructions:

1. Preheat a pan on medium heat. Grease with cooking spray.

2. In a large bowl, add in all-purpose flour, powdered cocoa, white sugar, baking powder and dash of salt. Stir well to mix.

3. In a small bowl, beat together eggs, pure vanilla and water. Whisk until lightly beaten. Pour this mixture into the flour mixture and beat again until just mixed. Add in the melted butter and miniature chocolate chips. Fold gently to incorporate.

4. Pour ¼ cup of the batter into the pan and spread thin. Cook, flipping when bubbles form on the surface.

5. Serve the crepes with a topping of powdered sugar and vanilla ice cream.

3. Sweet potato crepes

Simple and paleo, these sweet potato crepes can be combined with pretty much any sauce or side dish. Top with a poached egg and some cream cheese and you have a filling and healthy lunch.

Total time: 20m

Servings: 2

Ingredients:

- 1 sweet potato, grated
- 2 tbsp. Coconut flour
- 1 egg, beaten
- ½ tsp salt
- ¼ tsp dried parsley

Instructions:

1. Preheat your pan on high.

2. In a bowl, combine all ingredients.

3. Spoon the mixture into your pan and spread thin.

4. Cook until golden on both sides.

5. Serve and enjoy!

4. Oatmeal crepes

This is the perfect crepe dish that you can make whenever you need something healthy and filling to serve. Top these crepes off with fresh strawberries and blueberries for the tastiest results.

Total time: 15m

Servings: 6

Ingredients:

- 1 ½ cups of all-purpose flour
- 1 cup of rolled oats
- 1 tbsp. Of baking powder
- ½ tsp. Of ground cinnamon
- ¼ tsp. Of salt
- 2 eggs, beaten
- 1 ¾ cups of whole milk
- 6 tbsp. Of butter, melted
- 2 tbsp. Of light brown sugar

Instructions:

1. In a large bowl, combine all-purpose flour, rolled oats, ground cinnamon, baking powder and dash of salt. Stir well to mix.

2. In a separate bowl, add in the beaten eggs, whole milk, melted butter and light brown sugar. Whisk until evenly mixed.

3. Pour egg mixture into the flour mixture. Stir well until just mixed.

4. Preheat a pan on medium heat. Grease with cooking spray.

5. Pour ¼ cup of the batter into the pan and spread thin. Cover and cook for 2 minutes or until the crepes are golden. Repeat with the remaining crepe batter.

6. Serve crepes with a topping of syrup.

5. Coconut crepes with poppy and cinnamon cream

Delicious and sophisticated, these crepes are perfect for when you have guests over!

Total time: 30m

Servings: 4

Ingredients:

For the poppy and cinnamon cream

- 2 cups cream
- ¼ cup ready-made poppy seed filling
- 2 tbsp. Liquid honey
- Big pinch of ground cinnamon

For the crepes

- 1 ¾ stick butter
- ½ cup brown sugar
- 3 eggs
- 1 cup all-purpose flour
- ½ cup cornstarch
- 3/4 cup creamy coconut milk
- Pinch of salt
- 2 tbsp. Coconut liqueur
- Grated coconuts for garnish

Instructions:

1. For the poppy and cinnamon cream, put the quark, poppy seed filling, honey and cinnamon in a bowl and stir the ingredients to a smooth, creamy texture. Store the cream in a cool place until serving.

2. For the crepes, put butter into a mixing bowl and beat until soft. Add in sugar and beat until the mixture develops a uniform texture. Separate the eggs. Gradually add in the yolks. Mix the flour and cornstarch and gradually add to the batter alternately with the coconut milk.

3. Separately whip egg whites until stiff and fold into the batter with the coconut liqueur.

4. Put 2–3 tablespoons of batter for each crepe into a well-heated and greased pan and spread thin. Cook the crepes until golden brown.

5. Serve the crepes with the poppy and cinnamon cream and decorate with grated coconut.

6. Cheese crepes

Savory, cheesy, rich in flavor, and absolutely delicious, these chive and cheddar crepes make one simple and yet satisfyingly filling breakfast.

Total time: 20m

Servings: 6

Ingredients:

- 1 cup flour
- 2/3 cup shredded cheddar cheese
- 1 egg, white and yolk separated
- 2 tbsp. Yogurt
- 1 tbsp. Chopped chives
- ½ tbsp. Olive oil
- 1 cup milk
- ¼ tsp salt
- Pinch of pepper
- ½ tbsp. Baking powder

Instructions:

1. Beat egg white until stiff.

2. In another bowl, beat together the salt, yolk, milk, oil, yogurt, baking powder, pepper, and flour, until the mixture becomes smooth.

3. Fold in the egg white, cheese, and chives.

4. Pour 1/6 of the batter into a hot pan and cook for a few minutes.

5. Serve and enjoy!

7. S'more's crepes

With the help of this delicious dish, you will never have to go camping in order to enjoy homemade s'mores. Top off with extra marshmallows for the tastiest results.

Total time: 10m

Servings: 4

Ingredients:

- 1 basic buttermilk crepe recipe
- 4 graham crackers, cut into 8 squares
- ½ cup of miniature marshmallows
- ½ cup of chocolate chips

Instructions:

1. Prepare batter as directed in recipe 1.

2. To make the crepes, spoon 2 small rounds of batter onto a hot, greased pan, and spread thin. Cook for a couple of minutes. When bubbles start to form, flip over.

3. On one of the crepes, place 1 graham cracker square. Add 6 to 7 miniature marshmallows and 6 to 7 chocolate chips over the top. Cover with the second crepe and flatten slightly with a spatula until the chocolate is hot and melty.

4. Serve immediately, topped with more chocolate and marshmallows!

8. Banana bread crepes

The crepes are very convenient if you need something elegant to make. Most of the preparation for the crepes can be done the night before if you are tight on time.

Total time: 20m

Servings: 8

Ingredients:

- 4 tbsp. Of butter, melted
- 1 cup + 2 tbsp. Of whole milk
- 1 tsp. Of pure vanilla
- 2 cups of all-purpose flour
- 1 tbsp. Of light brown sugar
- 1 ½ tsp. Of active yeast
- ½ tsp. Of salt
- ½ tsp. Of powdered cinnamon
- ¼ tsp. Of powdered nutmeg
- 1/8 tsp. Of powdered ginger
- Dash of ground cloves
- 2 eggs, beaten lightly
- 1 cup of banana, mashed
- 2 tbsp. Of sour cream

Instructions:

1. In a bowl, add in the melted butter, whole milk and pure vanilla. Whisk well to mix. Set this mix aside.

2. In a separate bowl, add the all-purpose flour, light brown sugar, yeast, dash of salt, powdered cinnamon, powdered nutmeg, powdered ginger and dash of ground cloves. Stir well to mix.

3. Add milk mix into the flour mix. Stir well until just mix.

4. Preheat a pan. Grease with cooking spray.

5. Add ¾ cup of the brown batter onto the pan and spread. Cook, flipping once bubbles form on the surface.

6. Remove and repeat.

7. Serve with banana slices and nuts if desired!

9. Mac and cheese crepes

Kids are going to love these delicious mac and cheese crepes! They are perfect for a late brunch or even for dinner!

Total time: 40m

Servings: 10

Ingredients:

- 1, 6 to 8 ounce box of macaroni and cheese
- 2 tbsp. Of butter
- ¼ cup of whole milk
- 1 ½ cup of cheddar cheese, shredded
- 1 egg, beaten
- 1/3 cup of breadcrumbs

Instructions:

1. In a saucepan set over medium to high heat, fill with water. Allow to come to a boil. Add in the macaroni. Cook 8 -10 minutes or until tender. Drain the macaroni and set aside.

2. In a pan on low, add in 2 tablespoons of butter. Once melted, add in the whole milk and cheese pack from the box of macaroni and cheese. Whisk well until mixed.

3. Remove from heat.

4. Add in the cooked macaroni and 1 cup of shredded cheddar cheese. Stir well until melted.

5. Add in the egg and breadcrumbs. Stir well to incorporate.

6. Preheat a pan on the medium setting. Scoop ½ cup of the mac and cheese mix onto the preheated pan and spread as thin as possible. Cook for about 2 minutes until golden brown, before flipping and cooking for an additional 2 minutes. Remove and repeat.

7. Serve immediately.

10. Strawberry cheesecake crepes

This is the perfect crepe dish for you to make whenever you need something more festive.

Total time: 20m

Servings: 4

Ingredients:

- 1 to 2 cups of crepe mix
- ¾ cup of water
- 1/3 cup of vegetable oil
- 2 eggs, beaten
- 1, 3 to 4 ounce can of condensed milk
- 8 ounce pack of cream cheese, room temp
- 1 ¼ tbsp. of lemon juice
- 1/3 can of strawberry pie filling

Instructions:

1. Preheat a pan on medium heat. Grease with cooking spray.

2. In a blender, add in the crepe mix, beaten eggs and vegetable oil. Blend on lowest setting for 1 minute or until evenly mixed

3. Pour ¼ cup of the batter into the pan. Cover and cook for 2 minutes or until the crepes are golden.

4. Combine the cream cheese, lemon juice and condensed milk. Whisk until smooth in consistency.

5. Top the crepes with the cheesecake mixture and the strawberry pie filling over the top.

6. Serve immediately!

11. Dark chocolate crepe

This is a delicious belgian crepe dish you can make whenever you are craving chocolate. Dusted with powdered sugar, this is a dish everybody in your home will be begging for.

Total time: 40m

Servings: 6

Ingredients:

- 1 3/4 cups of all-purpose flour
- ½ cups of powdered cocoa, unsweetened
- ¼ cup of light brown sugar
- 2 tsp. baking powder
- 1 tsp. baking soda
- 1 tsp. salt
- 3 eggs, beaten and separated
- 2 1/4 cups of buttermilk
- ½ cup of extra virgin olive oil
- 1 tsp. pure vanilla
- 6 ounces of chocolate, bittersweet and chopped
- Butter, soft and for serving
- Maple syrup, for serving

Instructions:

1. Preheat oven to 250 degrees.

2. In a large bowl, combine flour, powdered unsweetened cocoa, light brown sugar, dash of salt, baking soda and powder. Stir well until evenly mixed.

3. Add in the beaten egg yolks, buttermilk, olive oil and pure vanilla. Stir until moist.

4. In a different bowl, add egg whites. Beat until peaks begin to form on the surface. Add the egg whites into the crepe mixture. Fold gently until just mixed.

5. Gently fold in the chocolate into the mixture.

6. Preheat pan to medium heat. Grease with cooking spray.

7. Pour ¼ cup of the batter into the pan. Cook for 2 minutes or until the crepes are golden brown, flipping once.

8. Serve the crepes with a topping of soft butter and syrup.

12. Pumpkin spice crepes

Banana and pumpkin spice yogurt give this recipe a warm and comforting taste that will satisfy absolutely everyone during holiday season. Serve topped with some extra bananas and honey.

Total time: 20m

Servings: 4

Ingredients:

- ½ tsp nutmeg
- 4 eggs
- ½ cup pumpkin spice yogurt
- 1 tsp ground ginger
- 1 tbsp. Cinnamon
- 2 cups oatmeal flour
- 3 bananas
- ¼ tsp ground cloves

Instructions:

1. Preheat your pan on high.

2. In a blender, combine all ingredients. Blend until smooth.

3. Pour mixture into the preheated pan and cook until golden.

4. Serve and enjoy!

13. Gingerbread crepes

Gingerbread in crepe form? Yes please!

Total time: 40m

Servings: 4

Ingredients:

- 1 stick butter
- ¼ cup sugar
- Pinch of salt
- 2 big pinches of ground cardamom
- Big pinch of ground ginger
- 5 eggs
- 2 cups wheat flour
- 1 cup light soured cream
- Icing sugar for dusting

Instructions:

1. Melt the butter in a pan and slightly brown. Remove the pan from the heat, pour the butter into a mixing bowl and leave to cool.

2. Add sugar, salt, cardamom and ginger to the cooled butter and mix the ingredients to a foamy texture. Gradually add the eggs and stir in. Sift in flour and fold into the batter before adding the soured cream.

3. Put 2–3 tablespoons of batter per portion in a well-heated and greased pan and cook the crepes until golden brown. Dust with icing sugar and serve immediately.

14. Chocolate chip crepes

This is a delicious and sweet crepe dish that you can make whenever you want to spoil your friends and family will something on the sweeter side.

Total time: 25m

Servings: 4

Ingredients:

- 1 3/4 cups of all-purpose flour
- ½ tsp. Of salt
- 1 ½ tbsp. Of white sugar
- 1 ½ tsp. Of baking soda
- 1 cup of miniature chocolate chips
- 2 cups of whole milk
- 2 tbsp. Of white vinegar
- 2 eggs, beaten
- ½ stick of butter, melted
- 1 tsp. Of pure vanilla

Instructions:

1. In a large bowl, add in the whole milk and white vinegar. Stir well to mix. Set aside for 10 minutes.

2. Combine all-purpose flour, white sugar, dash of salt, baking soda and miniature chocolate chips. Stir well to mix.

3. Preheat a pan on medium. Grease with cooking spray.

4. Add the beaten eggs, melted butter and pure vanilla into the milk and vinegar mixture. Whisk until evenly mixed. Pour into the flour mixture. Stir well until just mixed.

5. Pour ¼ cup of the batter into the pan. Cook until bubbles form on the surface and flip. Cook until done. Remove crepe and set aside on a large plate. Repeat with the remaining crepe batter.

6. Serve crepes with a topping of whipped cream and chocolate chips.

15. Oreo crepes

Another kid favorite, this recipe is great to make together with the family and is even greater when eaten together!

Total time: 40m

Servings: 6

Ingredients:

- 2 cups of all-purpose flour
- 10 oreos, crushed
- ¼ cup of light brown sugar
- 2 tsp. Of baker's style baking powder
- 1 tsp. Of baker's style baking soda
- 1 tsp. Of salt
- 3 eggs, beaten and separated
- 2 cups of buttermilk
- ½ cup of extra virgin olive oil
- 1 tsp. Of pure vanilla

Instructions:

1. Preheat the oven to 250 degrees.

2. Combine flour, crushed oreos, light brown sugar, dash of salt, baking powder and soda. Stir well until evenly mixed.

3. Add in the beaten egg yolks, buttermilk, olive oil and pure vanilla. Stir until moist.

4. In a separate bowl, add in the egg whites. Beat with an electric mixer until peaks begin to form on the surface. Add the egg whites into the crepe mixture. Fold gently until just mixed.

5. Preheat a pan on medium heat. Grease with cooking spray.

6. Pour ¼ cup of the batter into the pan and spread thin. Cook for 3 minutes or until the crepes are golden brown. Remove the crepe and set on a baking sheet. Keep warm in the preheated oven. Repeat with the remaining crepe batter.

7. Serve with fresh cream and more crushed oreos!!

16. Biscoff crepes

Gooey biscoff sauce on biscoff flavored crepes make this recipe simply to die for!

Total time: 40m

Servings: 6

Ingredients:

- 2 cups of all-purpose flour
- 10 biscoff biscuits, crushed
- ¼ cup of light brown sugar
- 2 tsp. baking powder
- 1 tsp. style baking soda
- 1 tsp. salt
- 3 eggs, beaten and separated
- 1 ¾ cup of buttermilk
- ¼ cup biscoff spread
- ½ cup of extra virgin olive oil
- 1 tsp. pure vanilla

Biscoff sauce –

- ¼ cup biscoff spread
- ¼ cup milk

Instructions:

1. Preheat the oven to 250 degrees.

2. To make the biscoff sauce, simple mix together the milk and biscoff spread until smooth. Set aside.

3. Combine flour, crushed biscoff, dash of salt, light brown sugar, baking powder and soda. Stir until evenly mixed.

4. Add in the beaten egg yolks, buttermilk, biscoff spread, olive oil and pure vanilla. Stir until moist.

5. In a separate bowl, add in the egg whites. Beat with an electric mixer until peaks begin to form on the surface. Add the egg whites into the crepe mixture. Fold gently until just mixed.

6. Preheat a pan on medium heat. Grease with cooking spray.

7. Pour ¼ cup of the batter into the pan and spread thin. Cook for 5 minutes or until the crepes are golden brown. Remove the crepe and set on a baking sheet. Keep warm in the preheated oven. Repeat with the remaining crepe batter.

8. Serve with fresh cream, biscoff sauce, and more crushed biscuits!

17. Apple pie crepes

Make this delicious crepe dish during the thanksgiving holiday as a spinoff on traditional apple pie! Serve with vanilla ice cream for the tastiest results.

Total time: 20m

Servings: 4

Ingredients:

- ¾ cup of whole-wheat flour
- ¾ cup of all-purpose flour
- 1 ½ tsp. baking powder
- ¼ cup coconut sugar
- ¼ cup apple sauce
- ½ cup coconut, shredded
- 1 tbsp. powdered flaxseed
- 3 tbsp. water
- 2 tbsp. sunflower oil
- 1 ½ cup almond milk
- 1 tbsp. powdered cinnamon
- 1 tsp. pure vanilla
- 1 tsp. corn starch
- Dash of sea salt

For syrup

- ½ cup of maple syrup
- ½ cup of apple juice
- 1 tbsp. Of powdered cinnamon
- ¼ tsp. Of powdered ginger

Garnish –

- Sliced apples, for serving
- Pecans, chopped and for serving

Instructions:

1. In a saucepan on med, add ingredients for the syrup. Cook for 3 minutes. Remove from heat and set aside.

2. In a bowl, add flaxseed and water. Whisk well to mix.

3. In a separate bowl, add whole-wheat flour, all-purpose flour, corn starch and baker's style baking powder. Stir well to mix.

4. In a different bowl, add apple sauce, pure vanilla, coconut, sunflower oil, almond milk, powdered cinnamon, sugar, flaxseed mix and dash of salt. Stir well to mix. Add into the flour mix and stir well until just mixed.

5. Set the batter aside to rest for 5 minutes.

6. Preheat a pan. Grease with cooking spray.

7. Pour ½ cup of the batter onto the pan. Cook for 5 minutes. Remove and repeat.

8. Serve the crepes with the apple slices and chopped pecans.

18. Nutella crepes

This delicious Nutella filled crepe recipe is guaranteed to be a crowd pleaser!

Total time: 10m

Servings: 4

Ingredients:

- 1 basic buttermilk crepe recipe
- ½ cup Nutella

Instructions:

1. Prepare batter as directed in recipe 1.

2. To make the crepes, spoon 2 small rounds of batter onto a hot, greased pan, and spread thin. Cook for 2 mins then flip over.

3. On one of the crepes, place 2 tbsp of Nutella. Cover with the second crepe and flatten slightly with a spatula.

4. Serve immediately, topped with wafers and more Nutella!

19. Ham and cheese hash brown crepes

If you love the hash browns, then these are the perfect breakfast crepes for you to make. Cheesy and delicious, these crepes will melt in your mouth with every bite.

Total time: 25m

Servings: 6

Ingredients:

- 1, 20 ounce pack of hash browns
- 8 ounces of ham, chopped
- 1 ½ cups of sharp cheddar cheese, shredded
- 3 eggs, beaten
- 2 cloves of garlic, minced
- 2 tbsp. Of parsley, chopped
- ½ tsp. Of dried thyme
- ¼ tsp. Of smoked paprika
- Dash of salt and black pepper

Instructions:

1. Heat up a pan on medium or high heat. Grease with cooking spray.

2. In a large bowl, add in the hash browns, chopped ham, shredded cheddar cheese, beaten eggs, minced garlic, chopped parsley, dried thyme and smoked paprika. Season this mixture with a dash of salt and black pepper. Stir well until evenly mixed.

3. Pour ¼ cup of the batter into the pan. Cook until bubbles form on the surface, then flip and continue cooking until done. Repeat with the remaining crepe batter.

4. Serve immediately.

20. French toast crepes

Who doesn't love French toast in the morning? But if you're looking for to jazz up your usual French toast breakfast, that's where these crepes come in!

Total time: 20m

Servings: 4

Ingredients:

- 5 eggs, beaten
- 1 French bread loaf, sliced
- 1 tsp vanilla
- 1 tbsp. Honey
- 2 tsp cinnamon

Instructions:

1. Whisk together the eggs, vanilla and honey.

2. Preheat your pan on high.

3. Dip the bread slices in egg and cook them in the pan for 2 minutes, or until golden.

4. Serve them sprinkled with cinnamon.

5. Enjoy!

21. Blueberry crepes

Although these blueberry crepes are irresistible delightful, they can be just as delicious if made with other berries or even another type of fruit. Feel free to tweak the recipe to your taste

Total time: 15m

Servings: 4

Ingredients:

- 2 cups flour
- ½ tsp baking soda
- 1 tsp baking powder
- ¼ tsp salt
- 2 eggs
- ¼ cup canola oil
- 1 tsp vanilla
- 2 cups buttermilk
- 1 cup blueberries
- ¼ cup sugar

Instructions:

1. Sift together the baking powder, soda, salt, and flour, in one bowl.

2. Whisk together the wet ingredients in another bowl.

3. Combine the two mixtures together.

4. Fold in blueberries, careful not to color the batter.

5. Pour batter into your preheated pan and cook for 4 minutes, until golden and crispy.

6. Serve and enjoy!

22. Tropical mango crepes

Mango nectar and coconut extract give these sweet crepes a tropical taste and flavor that will jumpstart your morning in a jiffy. Serve topped with some heavy cream and enjoy your breakfast.

Total time: 15m

Servings: 8

Ingredients:

- 1 cup mango nectar
- 4 ounces butter, melted
- 1 ½ tsp coconut extract
- 10 ounces self-rising flour
- 3 eggs, beaten
- 1 cup milk

Toppings –

- Fresh mango slices
- Fresh pineapple slices
- Whipped cream

Instructions:

1. Preheat your pan on high.

2. Whisk together all ingredients.

3. Spoon a bite of the batter into the pan and cook for a couple of minutes, until crispy and golden.

4. Serve with toppings and maple syrup!

23. Butter crepes with chocolate hazelnut filling

This crepe recipe combines delicious chocolate hazelnut filling with the tanginess of orange fruit!

Total time: 35m

Servings: 4

Ingredients:

For the filling

- 4 tbsp. Chocolate-hazelnut spread
- ½ cup milk
- 3 oranges

For the crepes

- 1 stick butter, softened
- 4 tbsp. Sugar
- 3 eggs
- 2 cups milk
- 1 cup flour
- 1 tsp baking powder
- Pinch of salt

Instructions:

1. Heat the chocolate-hazelnut spread and stir in the milk. Peel oranges and cut into thin slices.

2. For the crepes, whisk butter and sugar until creamy and then add the eggs singly. Add milk, flour, baking powder and salt and mix to a smooth batter without lumps. Put 2–3 tablespoons of batter per portion into the lightly greased and pre-heated pan and bake crepes until golden brown.

3. Spread half of the crepes with the chocolate-hazelnut cream and decorate with the orange slices. Lay the other crepes on top and dust with icing sugar.

24. Belgian chocolate crepes

Rich and chocolatey, these belgian crepes are excellent for brunch! Serve with a side of fresh whipped cream or vanilla ice cream for an indulgent treat!

Total time: 20m

Servings: 6

Ingredients:

- 1 ½ cups flour
- 1 cup sugar
- 2 eggs
- ¼ cup water
- 2/3 cup mini chocolate chips
- 2 tsp vanilla
- 10 tbsp. Butter, melted
- ½ cup cocoa powder, unsweetened
- 1 tsp salt
- 1 tsp baking powder

Instructions:

1. Preheat the pan on high.

2. Bea the wet ingredients with an electric mixer.

3. Combine the dry ingredients in a bowl and gradually beat them into the mixture.

4. Spoon a bit of the batter into the pan and cook for a few minutes until crispy.

5. Serve and enjoy!

25. Hazelnut crepes with cinnamon yogurt

This recipe is perfect for a chic brunch with all your friends! The cinnamon yogurt sauce adds a cool element to the crunchy crepe dish.

Total time: 25m

Servings: 4

Ingredients:

For cinnamon yogurt –

- 2 cups natural yoghurt
- 1 sachet vanilla sugar
- 1 tbsp. Ground cinnamon

For crepes –

- 1 cup low-fat quark
- 4 tbsp. Cooking oil
- ½ cup milk
- 4 tbsp. Sugar
- 2 eggs
- ½ cup wheat flour
- 1 sachet baking powder
- ½ cup sliced hazelnuts

Instructions:

1. For the cinnamon yoghurt, mix the yoghurt, vanilla sugar and cinnamon. Store the yoghurt in a cool place until serving.

2. For the crepes, put the quark, oil, milk, sugar and eggs into a mixing bowl and mix ingredients well. Add in flour and baking powder and stir into the batter. Add at least half of the hazelnuts and fold in.

3. Put 2–3 tablespoons of batter for each crepe into a well-heated and greased pan and spread flat. Bake the crepes until golden brown.

4. Serve the crepes with the cinnamon yoghurt decorated with the rest of the hazelnuts.

26. Maple and bacon crepes

Bacon is the epitome of breakfast and with the help of this delicious belgian crepe dish, you will be able to enjoy a filling and hearty breakfast.

Total time: 15m

Servings: 6

Ingredients:

- 1 ¼ cup of all-purpose flour
- 1 tbsp. Of baking powder
- 1 tbsp. Of white sugar
- ½ tsp. Of salt
- 3 eggs, beaten lightly
- 6 tbsp. Of butter, melted
- 1 ½ cup of whole milk
- 2 tsp. Of maple extract
- Candied bacon, chopped

Instructions:

1. In a bowl, combine flour, baking powder, white sugar and dash of salt. Stir well until evenly mixed.

2. In a different bowl, add in the beaten eggs, melted butter, whole milk and maple extract. Whisk until beaten lightly. Pour this mixture into the dry mixture. Stir until just mixed.

3. Add the candied bacon into the mixture and fold gently to mix.

4. Pour ¼ cup of the batter into the pan. Cook for 5 minutes or until the crepes are golden brown. Remove the crepe and set aside on a large plate. Repeat with the remaining crepe batter.

5. Serve the crepes with a topping of bacon and maple syrup!

27. Pecan pie crepes

These pecan pie crepes are just the thing you need in the morning to please your sweet tooth and pack you with feel good energy to last you until lunch.

Total time: 20m

Servings: 4-6

Ingredients:

- 1 ½ cups flour
- 1 cup chopped pecans
- 2 cups milk
- 1 tsp salt
- 1 tsp cinnamon
- ½ cup cornstarch
- ½ tsp baking soda
- ½ tsp nutmeg
- 2 tsp vanilla
- 2/3 cup oil
- 3 tbsp. Sugar
- 2 eggs
- 2 cups milk
- 1 tsp baking powder
- ½ cup cornstarch

Instructions:

1. Combine dry ingredients in a bowl.

2. Whisk together wet ingredients in another bowl.

3. Gently fold the two mixtures, but do not overmix.

4. Fold in the chopped pecans and let the batter sit for 10 minutes.

5. Meanwhile, preheat the pan.

6. Pour batter to the pan and cook the crepes until golden brown.

7. Serve and enjoy!

28. Fried chicken crepes

Crispy, crunchy, sweet, and savory! These fried chicken crepes are the perfect appetizer for a large party!

Total time: 40m

Servings: 24

Ingredients:

For chicken –

- Canola oil and for frying
- 1 ¼ cups of all-purpose flour
- 2 tbsp. Of cornstarch
- 1 tsp. Of cayenne pepper
- 1 tbsp. Of dried Italian seasoning
- 2 tsp. Of salt
- 1 tsp. Of black pepper
- 1 cup of buttermilk
- 1 ½ pound tenders (chicken), cut into small pieces
- Hot sauce, for serving

For crepes –

- 2 tsp. Of yeast
- ½ cup of warm water
- 1 ¾ cup of whole milk
- 6 tbsp. Of butter, melted
- 2 eggs
- ½ tsp. Of pure vanilla
- 2 cups of all-purpose flour
- 1 tbsp. Of white sugar
- Dash of salt
- Dash of cinnamon powder

Instructions:

1. Prepare the crepes. In a bowl, add in the yeast and warm water. Stir well to mix. Set aside to rest for 5 minutes or foamy.

2. In a separate bowl, add in the whole milk, melted butter, eggs and pure vanilla. Whisk light to mix. Add into the yeast mix.

3. In a different bowl, combine the flour, white sugar, dash of salt and powdered cinnamon. Stir to mix. Add into the milk mixture. Whisk well until smooth in consistency.

4. Cover and chill overnight.

5. Preheat a pan. Grease with cooking spray.

6. Pour ¼ cup of the crepe batter onto the iron. Cook for 5 minutes or until golden. Remove and repeat.

7. In a bowl, add in the cinnamon and white sugar for the topping. Stir well to mix. Toss the crepes with the topping until coated on all sides. Place onto a wire rack to rest.

8. In a pot on med heat, add 3 inches of canola oil. Heat oil until it reaches 350 degrees.

9. Prepare the chicken. In a bowl, add the flour, cayenne pepper, dried Italian seasoning, cornstarch, dash of salt and black pepper. Stir well to mix. In a separate bowl, add the buttermilk.

10. Toss chicken in the flour mix until coated on all sides. Dip into the buttermilk and roll again in the flour mix.

11. Drop the chicken into the hot oil. Fry for 5 minutes or until golden. Remove and transfer onto a plate lined with paper towels.

12. Serve the chicken with the crepes and a drizzle of hot sauce.

29. Pizza crepes

Looking for something creative and fun to make for breakfast this morning? These pizza crepes are perfect for breakfast, or lunch, or even dinner!

Total time: 15m

Servings: 4

Ingredients:

- 1 package of buttermilk biscuit dough
- ½ cup mini pepperoni
- 1 cup grated cheddar cheese
- 1/3 cup pizza sauce

Instructions:

1. Cut the dough into 8 equal pieces.

2. Stretch each of the pieces into circles.

3. Top half of the circler with the pizza fillings.

4. Place the other dough circles on top of the fillings, making sure that the fillings are tucked inside.

5. Cook the crepes on your heated pan and cook for about 3 minutes, or until golden.

6. Serve and enjoy!

30. Sand crepes with cinnamon sugar

These crepes are great for a school snack since they are sweet all on their own and do not require additional toppings!

Total time: 55m

Servings: 4

Ingredients:

- ½ cup coconut fat
- 1 cup sugar
- 1 sachet vanilla sugar
- Pinch of salt
- 4 eggs
- 1 cup wheat flour
- 2 tbsp. Corn starch
- ½ tsp baking powder

Cinnamon sugar -

- ½ tbsp. Cinnamon powder
- 1 tbsp. Sugar

Instructions:

1. Melt the coconut fat in a pan, pour into a mixing bowl and leave to cool slightly. Beat the almost solid coconut fat until smooth. Gradually add in sugar, vanilla sugar, and salt and mix together.

2. Then add the eggs singly. Mix flour with baking powder, and corn starch and gradually stir into the wet ingredients. Pour 2–3 tablespoons of batter into a well-heated and greased pan and spread flat. Bake the sand crepes until golden brown.

3. For the cinnamon sugar, mix the sugar with the cinnamon. Serve the crepes while still hot dusted with cinnamon sugar.

Conclusion

And there we have it! 30 fun and creative crepe recipes for you to try out. Chocolatey, savory or a combination of sweet and salty, we've got it all! And now, so do you! We truly hope you've enjoyed this book as much as we've had creating it!

About the Author

A native of Indianapolis, Indiana, Valeria Ray found her passion for cooking while she was studying English Literature at Oakland City University. She decided to try a cooking course with her friends and the experience changed her forever. She enrolled at the Art Institute of Indiana which offered extensive courses in the culinary Arts. Once Ray dipped her toe in the cooking world, she never looked back.

When Valeria graduated, she worked in French restaurants in the Indianapolis area until she became the head chef at one of the 5-star establishments in the area. Valeria's attention to taste and visual detail caught the eye of a local business person who expressed an interest in publishing her recipes. Valeria began her secondary career authoring cookbooks and e-books which she tackled with as much talent and gusto as her first career. Her passion for food leaps off the page of her books which have colourful anecdotes and stunning pictures of dishes she has prepared herself.

Valeria Ray lives in Indianapolis with her husband of 15 years, Tom, her daughter, Isobel and their loveable Golden Retriever, Goldy. Valeria enjoys cooking special dishes in her large, comfortable kitchen where the family gets involved in preparing meals. This successful, dynamic chef is an inspiration to culinary students and novice cooks everywhere.

Author's Afterthoughts

Thank you for Purchasing my book and taking the time to read it from front to back. I am always grateful when a reader chooses my work and I hope you enjoyed it!

With the vast selection available online, I am touched that you chose to be purchasing my work and take valuable time out of your life to read it. My hope is that you feel you made the right decision.

I very much would like to know what you thought of the book. Please take the time to write an honest and informative review on Amazon.com. Your experience and opinions will be of great benefit to me and those readers looking to make an informed choice.

With much thanks,

Valeria Ray

Made in the USA
Monee, IL
06 July 2024